Coolidge

jy
972
Rud

Mexico

by Jessica Rudolph

Consultant: Marjorie Faulstich Orellana, PhD
Professor of Urban Schooling
University of California, Los Angeles

BEARPORT
PUBLISHING

New York, New York

Credits

TOC, © Irafael/Shutterstock; 4, © milosk50/Shutterstock; 5T, © sisqopote/Shutterstock; 5B, © ChameleonsEye/Shutterstock; 7, © Rasjay/Thinkstock; 8, © Chris Curtis/Shutterstock; 9, © Alexandra Draghici/iStock; 10, © Jamie Robinson/Shutterstock; 11T, © fivespots/Shutterstock; 11B, © Noradoa/Shutterstock; 12, © robert cicchetti/Shutterstock; 13, © Marco Regalia/Shutterstock; 14–15, © Phototreat/iStock; 15, © Chad Zuber/Shutterstock; 16–17, © VICTOR TORRES/Shutterstock; 18–19, © Vladimir Korostyshevskiy/Shutterstock; 20, © Buddy Mays/Alamy; 21, © Jeff Greenberg/Gettyimages; 22, © Danita Delimont/Alamy; 23T, © Nataliya Arzamasova/Shutterstock; 23L, © KPG Payless2/Shutterstock; 23R, © Andris Tkacenko/Shutterstock; 24–25, © Marco Ugarte/AP/Corbis; 26T, © Jiri Hera/Shutterstock; 26B, © Yulia Davidovich/Shutterstock; 27, © Joshua Resnick/Shutterstock; 28, © Richard Ellis/Alamy; 29, © Judy Bellah/Alamy; 30 (T to B), © fourleaflove/Shutterstock, © Oleg_Mit/Shutterstock, © MarcusVDT/Shutterstock, and © Photo Work/Shutterstock; 31 (T to B), © abalcazar/iStock, © Marco Regalia/Shutterstock, © Marco Ugarte/AP/Corbis, © VICTOR TORRES/Shutterstock, and © Alexandra Draghici/iStock; 32, © Neftali/Shutterstock.

Publisher: Kenn Goin
Editor: J. Clark
Creative Director: Spencer Brinker
Design: Debrah Kaiser
Photo Researcher: Olympia Shannon

Library of Congress Cataloging-in-Publication Data

Rudolph, Jessica.
  Mexico / by Jessica Rudolph.
    pages cm. — (Countries we come from)
  Includes bibliographical references and index.
  Audience: Ages 4–8.
  ISBN 978-1-62724-853-2 (library binding) — ISBN 1-62724-853-6 (library binding)
  1. Mexico—Juvenile literature. I. Title.
  F1208.5.R84 2015
  972—dc23

                              2015004744

For more information, write to Bearport Publishing Company, Inc., 45 West 21st Street, Suite 3B, New York, New York 10010. Printed in the United States of America.

10 9 8 7 6 5 4 3 2 1

Contents

This Is Mexico 4

Fast Facts 30

Glossary 31

Index 32

Read More 32

Learn More Online 32

About the Author 32

This Is Mexico

WARM

Colorful

LIVELY

Mexico is a country in North America.

Most of Mexico is surrounded by water.

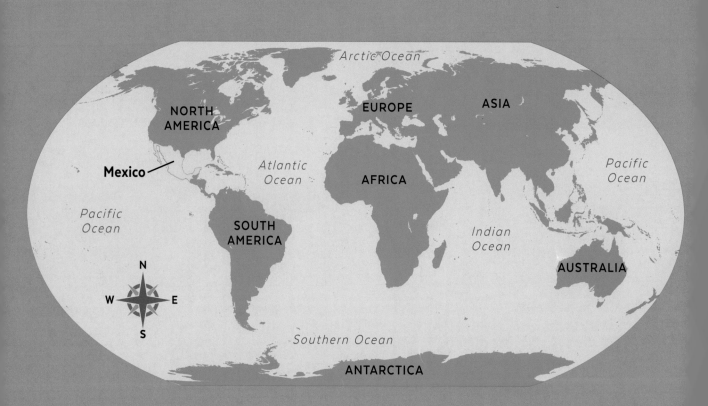

People surf at Mexico's many beaches.

Most of Mexico is warm all year.

Many plants grow in the warm weather.

Spiky cactuses grow in Mexico's deserts.

Organ pipe cactuses can live more than 150 years.

Tall trees grow in **rain forests**.

Thousands of kinds of animals live in Mexico. Spider monkeys live in trees.

Gila monsters dig homes under the ground.

These lizards have a poisonous bite.

Monarch butterflies spend winter in Mexico. After winter, most of them travel north to the United States.

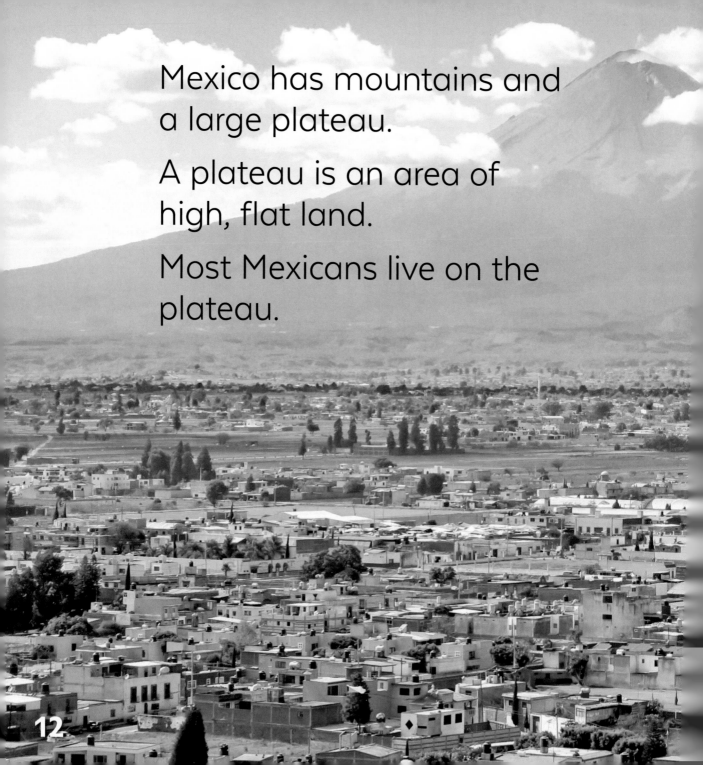

Mexico has mountains and a large plateau.

A plateau is an area of high, flat land.

Most Mexicans live on the plateau.

Mexico also has more than 3,000 volcanoes. Sometimes they **erupt**.

Mexico City is the country's largest city.

It's also the **capital**.

Nearly nine million people live in Mexico City. More people live there than in New York City.

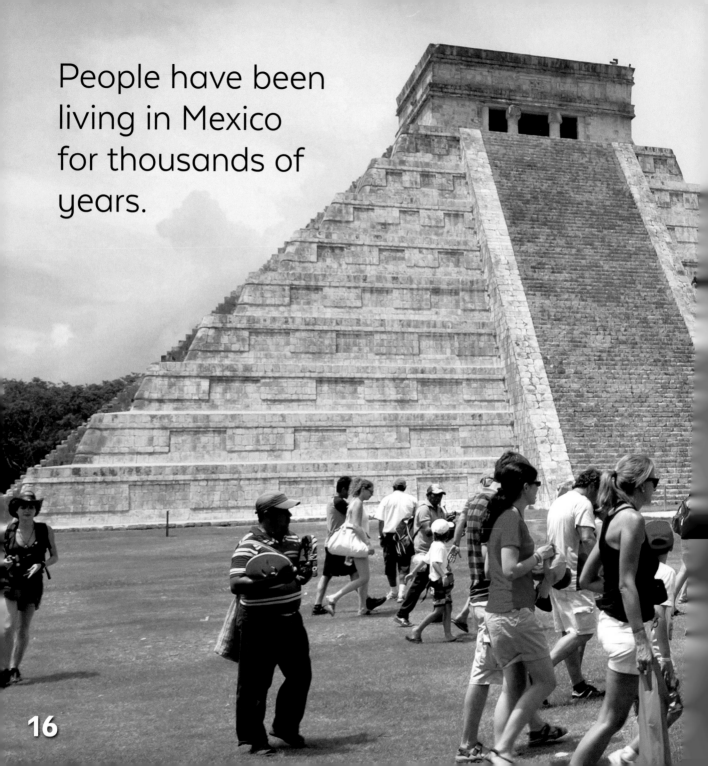

People have been living in Mexico for thousands of years.

Indians, such as the Maya and the Aztecs, built large cities.

Chichen Itza was a Maya city. A huge **pyramid** stands there. Many people visit it.

The Spanish came to Mexico in the 1500s.

They ruled for hundreds of years.

Mexico is no longer ruled by Spain.

Today, most Mexicans are part Spanish and part Indian.

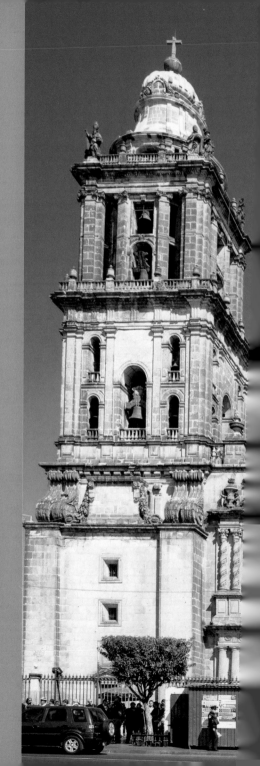

The Spanish built many churches. Some of them are still used today.

Spanish and many Indian languages are spoken in Mexico.

How do you say *please* in Spanish?

Por favor (PORE fah-VORE)

Mexico is the largest Spanish-speaking country in the world.

This is how you say *thank you*:
Gracias (GRAH-see-uhss)

Mexicans have many kinds of jobs.

Some people work in factories.

workers building a car

Other people work on farms.

They grow foods like avocados and cacao.

avocados

Cacao pods grow on trees. Chocolate is made from the pods.

chocolate

23

Many towns have plazas.

These are outdoor spaces where people can relax or see friends.

Mariachi bands often play music in the plazas.

Mariachi musicians
play instruments such
as violins, trumpets,
and guitars.

What foods do Mexicans like?

Many people eat tacos.

Tacos are made with thin bread called tortillas.

The tortillas can be folded around meat, cheese, and vegetables.

For a treat, some people drink spiced hot chocolate.

tacos

Mexicans celebrate lots of holidays.

The Day of the Dead is in November.

People honor dead friends and family on this day.

flowers and candles on graves

People decorate graves on the Day of the Dead. Some dress up like skeletons.

Fast Facts

Capital city: Mexico City

Population of Mexico: 122 million

Main language: Spanish

Money: Peso

Major religions: Christian and American Indian religions

Neighboring countries: United States, Guatemala, and Belize

Cool Fact: Soccer is the most popular sport in Mexico—and the world. In Mexico and many other countries, soccer is called fútbol (FOOT-bole).

capital (KAP-uh-tuhl) a city where a country's government is based

erupt (i-RUPT) to send out lava, ash, steam, and gas from a volcano

mariachi (mahr-ee-AH-chee) a type of Mexican street music played with trumpets, guitars, and violins

pyramid (PIHR-uh-mid) a stone structure with a square base and triangular sides

rain forests (RAYN FOR-ists) warm areas of land covered with trees and other plants, where lots of rain falls

31

Index

animals 10–11
food 23, 26–27
holidays 28–29
Indians 17, 18, 30

jobs 22–23
languages 20–21, 30
Mexico City 14–15, 30
plants 8–9

plateau 12
plazas 24–25
Spanish people 18
volcanoes 13

Read More

Heiman, Sarah. *Mexico ABCs: A Book About the People and Places of Mexico (Country ABCs).* Minneapolis, MN: Picture Window Books (2003).

Landau, Elaine. *Mexico (A True Book).* New York: Children's Press (2008).

Learn More Online

To learn more about Mexico, visit
www.bearportpublishing.com/CountriesWeComeFrom

About the Author

Jessica Rudolph lives in Connecticut. She has edited and written many books about history, science, and nature for children.